TURN TO THE
BACK FOR A HELPFUL
NAVIGATION GUIDE
FOR PARENTS

More support materials available on our
website flyingstartbooks.com/parents

What Feels Cold?
and Other Stories

A Red Rocket Readers Collection

Contents

TURN TO THE BACK FOR A HELPFUL NAVIGATION GUIDE FOR PARENTS

More support materials available on our website flyingstartbooks.com/parents

Collected edition first published in 2018 by Red Rocket Readers, an imprint of Flying Start Books Ltd.
Individual tltles first published in 2006 by Red Rocket Readers, an imprint of Flying Start Books Ltd.
13/45 Karepiro Drive, Auckland 0932, New Zealand.

What Feels Cold? Story © Pam Holden
Photographs supplied by Photolibrary
Come to the Library. Story © Pam Holden
Photographs supplied by Jupiter Unlimited, Photolibrary and Stock Central
Opposites. Story © Pam Holden
Photographs supplied by Stock Central, Photolibrary, iStock Photo and Jupiter Unlimited
What Can You See? Story © Pam Holden
Photographs supplied by Thinkstock Photos and Photolibrary
What Feels Sticky? Story © Pam Holden
Photographs supplied by Jupiter Unlimited and Stock Central
What is Fun? Story © Pam Holden
Photographs supplied by Photolibrary
What is Noisy? Story © Pam Holden
Photographs supplied by Photolibrary
What is Quiet? Story © Pam Holden
Photographs supplied by Stock Central and Jupiter Unlimited
ISBN 978-1-77654-197-3
Printed in India

What Feels Cold?

written by Pam Holden

The snow feels cold

The wind feels cold.

The ice feels cold.

The iceberg
feels cold.

refrigerator s cold.

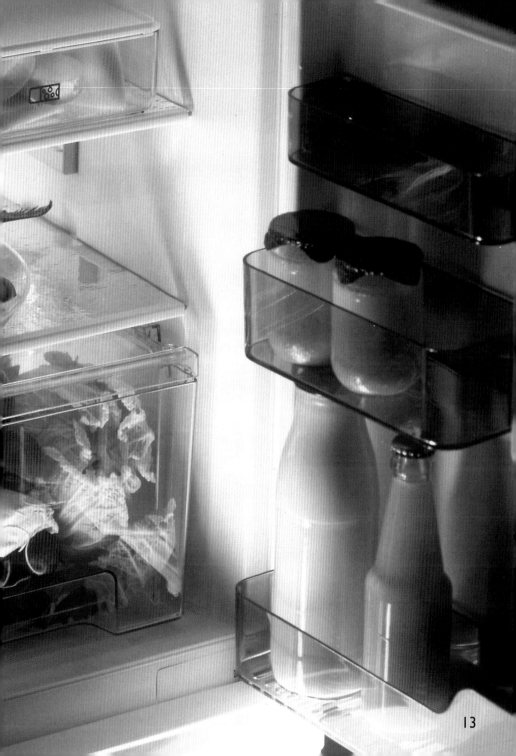

The ice-cream feels cold.

The snowman feels cold.

The snowball feels
very cold!

Come to the Library

written by Pam Holden

You can read
about animals.

You can read
about the world.

You can read
about the sea.

You can read
about space.

You can read
about the jungle.

You can read about the weather.

You can read
about the desert.

You can read about dinosaurs. Roar!

Opposites

written by Pam Holden

This is hot.

But this is cold.

This is big.

But this is little.

This is up.

But this is down.

This is fast.

But this is slow.

This is old.

But this is new.

This is happy.

This is dry.

But this is wet.

This is wet, too!

What Can You See?

written by Pam Holden

Can you see
1 snake?

Can you see 2 tigers?

Can you see
3 elephants?

Can you see
4 monkeys?

Can you see 5 lions?

Can you see 6 zebras?

Can you see
7 giraffes?

64

Can you see
8 hippos?
1 2 3 4 5 6 7 8!

What Feels Sticky?

written by Pam Holden

This glue feels sticky.

This honey feels sticky.

This spider web
feels sticky.

This mud
feels sticky.

This orange juice
feels sticky.

This toothpaste
feels sticky.

This dough
feels sticky.

This paint feels very sticky. Ooops!

What is Fun?

written by Pam Holden

A clown is fun.

A story is fun.

A game is fun.

A swing is fun.

A dance is fun.

A rollercoaster is fun.

A bike ride is fun.

A party is fun, too!

What is Noisy?

written by Pam Holden

A trumpet is noisy.

A bulldozer is noisy

A drum is noisy.

A fire truck is noisy.

A storm is noisy.

A waterfall is noisy.

A helicopter
is noisy.

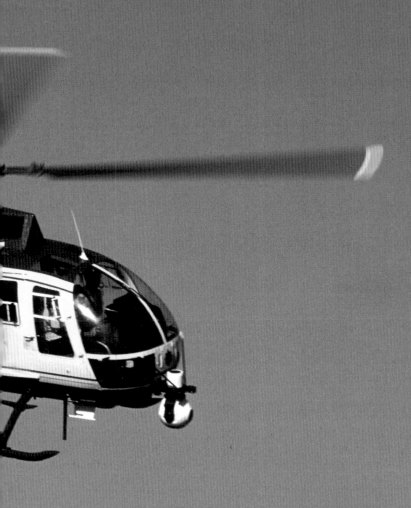

A band is very noisy!

What is Quiet?

written by Pam Holden

A mouse is quiet.

A giraffe is quiet.

A spider is quiet.

A rabbit is quiet.

A snail is quiet.

A fish is quiet.

A snake is quiet.

A snake is not quiet SSsssssssss!

NAVIGATION GUIDE FOR PARENTS

Support and enhance the work your child is doing at school with additional practice at every level.

Follow these steps to get them off to a flying start with literacy and learning:

1. **Picture walk and talk before you read** to introduce each story, its title and what it is about. Take a page-by-page picture walk to introduce new concepts and talk about what might happen in the story.

2. **Read together every day.** Red Rocket Readers Collections are ideal for a week of home reading practice, reading one story each day.

3. **Choose the right books!** A funny story, an interesting topic, and the right reading level – children need books that they can manage successfully and enjoy.

4. **Be positive!** It's essential that early learning-to-read experiences are positive, so praise all efforts.

These vital steps will set children up for early success!

Read more at flyingstartbooks.com/parents

INTRODUCING THE STORIES IN THIS COLLECTION

"This story is called **What Feels Cold?** It's about things that are cold. What are some things that feel cold when you touch them? What other things are cold? Is there something cold in your home?"

Sight words: **cold   the   very**

"This story is called **Come to the Library.** It's about the things you can read about in the library. Do you go to the library? What do you do there? Which books do you choose? Do you take some books home? What do you like to read about?"

Sight words: **can   come   the   to   you**

"This story is called **Opposites.** It's about things that are opposites. Do you know what we mean when we say opposites? That means they are quite different to each other. Tall is the opposite to short. Late is the opposite to early. What is the opposite to awake?"

Sight words: **big   but   down   is   little   this   up**

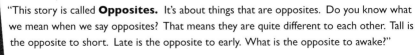

"This story is called **What Can You See?** It's about counting different kinds of animals. Are you good at counting? How many animals can you count in each picture? You need to count very carefully!"

Sight words: **can   see   you**

"This story is called **What Feels Sticky?** It's about some things that feel sticky? Have you ever got so hot that your clothes felt sticky? What makes you get sticky fingers sometimes? Do you use sticky tape or stickers? What else feels sticky?"

Sight words: **this   very**

"This story is called **What is Fun?** It's about things to do that are fun. Everyone likes to have fun. What do you like to do that is fun? Who helps us to have fun?"

Sight words: **A   is   too**

"This story is called **What is Noisy?** It's about some things that are noisy. Can you hear any noises now? What are some things that are very noisy? Do you make a lot of noise sometimes? How?"

Sight words: **A   is   very**

"This story is called **What is Quiet?** It's about some things that are quiet. Can you whisper with a very quiet voice? Some animals don't make any noise at all. Do you know which animals have no voice? What else is very quiet?"

Sight words: **A   is   not**

Look For Other Titles Available Now:

A BOOK FOR EVERY READER!

Learning to read is a complex process, that draws upon an extensive knowledge base and repertoire of strategies. Each essential step must be secure before progressing to the next level.

Award winning Red Rocket Readers feature controlled-language that is reading level appropriate. With a 50/50 split of fiction and non-fiction texts, supported by attractive illustrations for fiction and stunning photography supporting the non-fiction texts, there's a book for every reader.

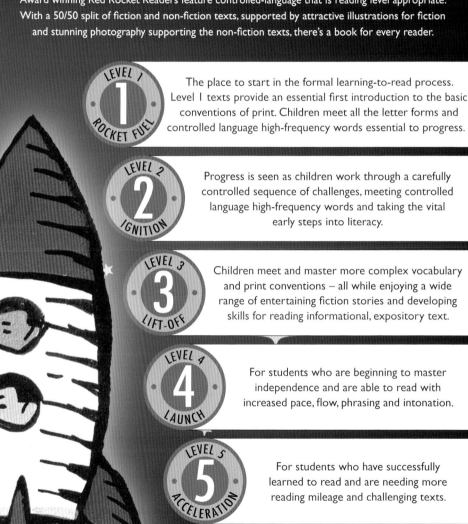

LEVEL 1 — 1 ROCKET FUEL
The place to start in the formal learning-to-read process. Level 1 texts provide an essential first introduction to the basic conventions of print. Children meet all the letter forms and controlled language high-frequency words essential to progress.

LEVEL 2 — 2 IGNITION
Progress is seen as children work through a carefully controlled sequence of challenges, meeting controlled language high-frequency words and taking the vital early steps into literacy.

LEVEL 3 — 3 LIFT-OFF
Children meet and master more complex vocabulary and print conventions – all while enjoying a wide range of entertaining fiction stories and developing skills for reading informational, expository text.

LEVEL 4 — 4 LAUNCH
For students who are beginning to master independence and are able to read with increased pace, flow, phrasing and intonation.

LEVEL 5 — 5 ACCELERATION
For students who have successfully learned to read and are needing more reading mileage and challenging texts.

LEVEL 6 — 6 BOOST
Increase student's reading ability and boost their confidence by engaging interest, using a variety of appealing text types and genres.